HAGAR

BEFORE THE OCCUPATION

HAGAR

AFTER THE OCCUPATION

HAGAR
BEFORE THE OCCUPATION

HAGAR
AFTER THE OCCUPATION

poems by

AMAL AL-JUBOURI

Translated by Rebecca Gayle Howell with Husam Qaisi

Foreword by Alicia Ostriker

ALICE JAMES BOOKS TRANSLATION SERIES
FARMINGTON, MAINE

10 9 8 7 6 5 4 3 2 1

Alice James Books are published by Alice James Poetry Cooperative,
Inc., an affiliate of the University of Maine at Farmington.

ALICE JAMES BOOKS

238 MAIN STREET

FARMINGTON, ME 04938

www.alicejamesbooks.org

Library of Congress Cataloging-in-Publication Data

Jubouri, Amal.
  [Hajar qabla al-ihtilal, Hajar ba'da al-ihtilal. English & Arabic]
  Hagar before the occupation, Hagar after the occupation : poems /
by Amal al-Jubouri ; translated by Rebecca Gayle Howell with Husam
Qaisi.
    p. cm.
  ISBN 978-1-882295-89-0
  I. Howell, Rebecca Gayle. II. Qaisi, Husam. III. Title.
  PJ7840.U255H3513 2011
  808.81--dc22
                                        2011015821

Alice James Books gratefully acknowledges support from individual
donors, private foundations, the University of Maine at Farmington
and the National Endowment for the Arts. ❦

CONTENTS

باب الأناشيد / The Cantos Chapter

ACKNOWLEDGMENTS

Grateful acknowledgment is made to the editors of the following publications, in which these versions first appeared, sometimes in earlier forms:

Border Crossing: "Honor Before the Occupation," "Honor After the Occupation," "Photographs Before the Occupation," "Photographs After the Occupation."

Catch Up: Louisville: "My Soul Before the Occupation," "My Soul After the Occupation."

Connotation Press: An Online Artifact: "My Daughter Before the Occupation," "My Daughter After the Occupation," "My Husband Before the Occupation," "My Husband After the Occupation."

Ecotone: "Hagar Before the Occupation," "Baghdad Before the Occupation."

Great River Review: "Men Before the Occupation," "Men After the Occupation," "Regret Before the Occupation," "Regret After the Occupation," "Bones Before the Occupation," "Bones After the Occupation."

Hayden's Ferry Review: "Eid Before the Occupation," "Eid After the Occupation," "Soccer Before the Occupation," "Soccer After the Occupation," "Death Before the Occupation," "Death After the Occupation."

The Massachusetts Review: "My Body Before the Occupation," "My Body After the Occupation," "My Grave Before the Occupation," "My Grave After the Occupation," "My Mouth Before the Occupation," "My Mouth After the Occupation," "My Loneliness Before the Occupation," "My Loneliness After the Occupation," "Love Before the Occupation," "Love After the Occupation."

Poetry Daily: "My Body Before the Occupation," "My Body After the Occupation," "My Grave Before the Occupation," "My Grave After the Occupation," "My Mouth Before the Occupation," "My Mouth After the Occupation," "My Loneliness Before the Occupation," "My Loneliness After the Occupation," "Love Before the Occupation," "Love After the Occupation."

Gratitude to the following for their support: Alice James Books; the Fine Arts Work Center in Provincetown, MA; the Kentucky Foundation for Women; The Drew University Low-Residency MFA Program in Poetry & Poetry in Translation; and Morehead State University. Especially: Dr. Salih J. and Amal Altoma, Julia Bouwsma, Arwen Donahue, George Eklund, Frank Giampietro, Barbara Hausman, Chris Holbrook, Fadel Jabr, Joan Larkin, Anne Marie Macari, Mihaela Moscaliuc, Margaret Murphy, Jeremy Paden, Vemihan Qaisi, Carey Salerno, Salvatore Scibona, Adel Sheikhly, Roger Skillings, Griffin and Sarah Wylie VanMeter, Michael Waters, Ellen Doré Watson, and Crystal Wilkinson.

FOREWORD

As I began reading *Hagar Before the Occupation / Hagar After the Occupation*, two quotations sprang to mind, both written by brilliant stylists for whom the relation of art to politics and history stood at the core of their creativity. Dmitri Shostakovich—praising the poet Yevgeny Yevtushenko's poem "Babi Yar," about the covered-up massacre of the Jews of Kiev in World War II, which the composer had used as text for his thirteenth symphony—declared in his memoirs: *People knew about Babi Yar before Yevtushenko's poem, but they were silent. And when they read the poem, the silence was broken. Art destroys silence.* The requirement of all totalitarian regimes, all police states, is silence. But art destroys silence. The book you hold in your hands clearly serves that need. It defies "the demise of manhood," "the indecent face of death," "the tyrants' violence," "the invaders' grunts." The second quote is Walter Benjamin's, describing how human culture is created and sustained by conquest: *There is no document of civilization that is not at the same time a document of barbarism.* This is a more complex statement. It asks us to stand outside the master narratives of our own culture; it takes into account the ambiguity, the doubleness, of all art; it demands that the author engage in self-questioning. It implies doubling, doubling back . . . and, perhaps, absurdity.

The poet Amal al-Jubouri, in exile but still in love with her "wounded master" Iraq, does not permit herself to flinch from these demands. Muteness tempts her, barbarism haunts her; nevertheless she speaks. To experience the deceptive simplicity and austerity of her language and syntax, is to become complicit in doubleness . . . and, surely, absurdity.

How, for example, should we read the provocative title of *Hagar Before the Occupation / Hagar After the Occupation?* This doubling might evoke the "before / after" images that saturate commercial culture, inviting us to buy products that will improve our complexions, grow our hair, or take away our fat and make us more sexually appealing as products ourselves. Before and After then would mean Bad versus Good. To the reader aware that the Occupation refers to the conquest and continued occupation of the author's country, Iraq, by foreign military forces (in particular American and British), the title might lead us to expect a depiction of a happy time followed by an unhappy one. Before and After then would mean Good versus Bad.

The first pair of poems in the book will immediately disabuse the reader of both these expectations. We are not presented with crude opposites. Here is a "Before," in a single line:

My Country Before the Occupation

Passport—travel not permitted

With this simple gesture the poet evokes a regime of fear, a regime that holds its citizens captive. We register the bureaucratic idiom that refuses human responsibility. Who or what permits or fails to permit? Bureaucracy never discloses such information. We register, as well, the absurdity of a document that exists for the purpose of travel, existing to prevent it. Yet the shining word "travel" evokes all we may desire in a state of freedom, even imagination.

The following poem offers us another kind of absurdity, combined (at least for a non-Iraqi reader) with mystery:

My Country After the Occupation

Passport for my Philippino maid—

Red stamped:
NOT VALID TO IRAQ

At least two scenarios offer themselves. The poet's maid is in
Iraq illegally, which means people have been bribed. Or the
poet and her maid are in exile. We are not to discover which.
Either way, "Red stamped" evokes violence in its adjective and
in its verb. And again, the source and reason for the restriction
remain bureaucratically sealed. A few pairs later, different sorts of
absurdity begin to surface:

My Neighbor Before the Occupation

Um-Hayder keened for a two-dollar raise
In her husband's check

But slept with the front door open
So the breeze could blow fresh from the garden next door
Tended by cooks for the Republican Palace

There's a bit of comedy here, as though smelling what drifted
from Saddam Hussein's gardens might substitute for actual food.
Yet the pathos of the minimal wish adjacent to an image of impe-
rial splendor represents an entire social structure of power and
powerlessness. What follows may be as surprising to the reader as
to Um-Hayder herself. Four quick lines encapsulate a Baghdad
riven by sectarian violence in which neighbor will betray neighbor

for a pittance, and in which to be a Shi'ite rather than a Sunni is to be at once empowered and endangered.

My Neighbor After the Occupation

Now her husband's check is twenty dollars fatter,
But Um-Hayder can't risk breathing her new neighbor's
    air—
It will sense her Shi'ite scent, hidden for decades
Just to have one dollar more

Another kind of doubling inhabits the name Hagar. In the Book of Genesis, the banished Hagar and her son Ishmael are saved from death in the desert by angelic intervention—but then we hear no more of them. Ishmael for Jews becomes the quintessential Other to Isaac, and in today's Israel the name is still used as a synonym for "Arab." In Hebrew, the name Hagar is a cognate for Ha-ger, the stranger. But in Islamic tradition, Hagar is the legitimate wife of Ibrahim, and Ismail his legitimate beloved son. Sent into the desert by Sarah's jealousy and by God's will, according to Islamic legend, Hagar becomes a founder of the holy city of Mecca and is an ancestress of the Prophet. Her name, pronounced in Arabic with a soft g, Hajar, is honored in the *hajj*, the pilgrimage every Muslim is expected to take to worship at Mecca. Speaking in the voice of Hagar today, the poet is both exiled stranger and sacred ancestress. She is the ultimate outsider / insider. Her body is both "Ammunition for wars to come" and "A loaf of hot bread // aching to be eaten." Before the Occupation, her mouth "tried to say *no*, but couldn't / I was afraid." After the occupation, her mouth "Shouts No! Fearless," but truth is "already gone // Exiled with God's tongues."

The poet's soul, her grave, her daughter and husband, the Tigris, Freedom, Honor, Regret, Love, Soccer, Bones, Baghdad—these are among the objects, sublime and profane, which al-Jubouri targets Before and After. War is a constant: "War is a whore / She doesn't care about anyone / Just her price, paid up-front." Loneliness is "This market of conscience . . . looted." Struck by the force and intimacy of al-Jubouri's language, we may experience the beauty of her writing as redemptive in the face of despair. Shockingly, toward the close of the book, in a long poem entitled "Poetry After the Occupation" al-Jubouri denounces poetry itself as "a spy speaking half-truths . . . the lowest of gods . . . Defeated . . . a pygmy . . . " and even a prison, "this Abu Ghraib / where all are sadists // the inmates, jailers the jailors, inmates / of your strange promises." As an American wedded to optimism, I hear this denunciation, this renunciation, as the cry of a betrayed lover who secretly still craves the return of the promise of youth. Yet is this not the clearest imperative for a poet in our times—to declare the powerlessness of art in the face of history's overwhelming brutality, while continuing stubbornly to create that art?

Epigrammatic and riddling, impassioned and furious, crystalline in its irony, *Hagar Before the Occupation / Hagar After the Occupation* evokes a woman's body and mind rooted in geography, history, faith, art, and the bitterness of "All the wars, one war / One terror." It is the most exciting and original book of pure poetry I have read in a long time. The Iraqi poet Amal al-Jubouri, beautifully translated by Rebecca Gayle Howell, will immediately take her place alongside Neruda and Tsvetaeva and Celan—poets of exile, yes, and poets of difficult truth.

—Alicia Ostriker

TRANSLATOR'S PREFACE

If you are One
and your teachings are One
why did you inscribe our infancy in the Torah
and adorn our youth in the Gospels
only to erase all that in your final book?
Why did you draw those of us who acknowledge your
    oneness into disagreement
Why did you multiply in us, when you are the one
    and only One

>   —Amal al-Jubouri
>   "The Veil of Religions"
>   (translated by Seema Atalla)

I decided to translate Amal al-Jubouri based on this one poem,
which she wrote in response to September 11, 2001. The Iraqi poet
who could write this poem without recoil, I thought, might be
writing equally fearless poetry about the American invasion and
occupation of her country. And so I encountered al-Jubouri one
poem at a time, one line at a time, much the same as you will.

Amal al-Jubouri is a member of the so-called 80's Generation,
a group of Iraqi poets that includes Jawad al-Hattab, Fadel Jabr,
Dunya Mikhail, and Adnan al-Sayegh. These poets came of age
during Iraq's invasion of Iran in 1980 and have matured through
an era of what must feel like unending war. Al-Jubouri's first book,

Wine from Wounds, was published when she was nineteen years old; at the same time, she was becoming an outspoken journalist. Like many members of the Iraqi intelligentsia, she sought refuge during the embargo, moving to Germany in 1997. She returned to Iraq after the Ba'ath Party's fall in 2003 and lived there during the war.

In this collection, al-Jubouri has called upon the matriarch of Islam, Hagar, as her muse. In the original narrative, Hagar, abandoned to the desert of her exile, runs between Safa and Marwa pleading to God for water. In al-Jubouri's adaptation of the story, Hagar's desperation is suspended in time. In the preface poem, an address to Iraq, the poet writes:

> Hagar paces without end between
> Safa — your soul
> and Marwa — your life
>
> The Tigris is her Mecca   The Euphrates, her Ka'ba
> Baghdad, her bond   unbreaking
>
> My lord — your love
> her only identity and priest

As Hagar runs between the two mountains, so the poet runs between the years of the embargo and the years of the Occupation. As Hagar begs for the grace that water will spring from the desert, so al-Jubouri prays for unity during war.

❦

This book was translated in collaboration with Husam Qaisi, a Palestinian American and a devout Muslim, who has much more English than I have Arabic, and who acted as the literal translator for this project.

While English grammar depends on word order, Arabic depends on changes, or "inflections," in the words themselves. Linguists call languages such as Arabic, Latin, or Sanskrit "efficient" for their ability to distribute meaning more concisely than languages that use less flexible syntax. While English is rife with synonyms, Arabic uses word roots to carry a multitude of meanings, clarified through context. Consequently, a poet skilled in open Arabic verse can write with a certain compression.

For these reasons, Qaisi and I began our translations with tables that broke the original Arabic poems into cells and rows of words and lines. Qaisi would build them, alternating the Arabic rows with corresponding ones in English; he then provided other English synonyms, context clues, and any historical background in notes. We stepped back from the more traditional methods of translation, so that I could see each poem in its most essential components before ordering it grammatically. By taking this precaution, I was allowed a closer relationship with the Arabic and with al-Jubouri's choices within each poem.

How does one choose between the preservation of a cultural heritage and the job of interpreting it? I found the path marked by compromises. Al-Jubouri—like her early influence Emily Dickinson—uses the rhetoric of her surrounding religion to question extreme ideology. She and I chose to augment the effect of her religious imagery by occasionally using Judeo-Christian expressions more common in English-language literature. We used words like *hymn* or phrases like *kingdom come* when it was possible to do so without causing distraction. More often I stayed close to the original idiom even when a note would be required, and sometimes I had recourse for transliterations like *al-Sayed* and *Nikah Misyar*.

Al-Jubouri often grounds her language in near rhymes. Hagar, as established in the foreword to this book, is pronounced in Arabic with a soft /g/ sound and shares its root with "hajj," which means "pilgrimage." For the Arabic reader, al-Jubouri's title implies the conflicts of diaspora. In "Poetry After the Occupation," she calls poetry both "Abu Ghraib," the military prison made infamous by the American torture program; and "abu gharib," literally "father of strangers." Needless to say, her music was largely untranslatable; instead, I stayed faithful to the poems' most distinguishing element: compression—the control she asserts over the chaos of her subject matter. While Arabic tolerates repetition due to its linguistic compression, English does not; I omitted phrases or lines where the recurrence was not essential to structure. In order to provide a framework for these decisions, the line breaks, stanza breaks, and punctuation are largely of my choosing. The English versions sometimes have a greater line count than the Arabic poems, a consequence of using additional stanzas and short lines to cast a relatively inefficient target grammar. This effect is most obvious in the collection's longest poem, "Poetry After the Occupation."

All departures from the original poems are, in her words, "Amal al-Jubouri Approved." Whenever I would go too far from the source poem, Husam would correct me. If we hadn't gone far enough, Amal would correct us both.

✻

Since 2003, an unprecedented portion of Iraq's intelligentsia has left the country. We are now facing each other anew. As American writers and readers of poetry, we would be wise to welcome a poetic tradition of such antiquity and weight.

This book is a collaboration, informed by argument and compromise. Which is fitting, since the poems themselves move toward unity, but only by way of the good fight. In July 2010 Amal and I traveled to New York together. We visited the Statue of Liberty, a first for both of us. While waiting in line, Amal struck up a conversation with an American woman, a Republican, a Bush supporter. They debated what had led us to war. The need for oil or the need for democracy? An hour later—still inside the Statue, all of us impatient with the day's stale humidity—they arrived at their conclusion: it no longer mattered what had led us to war. We were at war.

—Rebecca Gayle Howell

" ماأعطي بالذل يجلب العار"

مثل سومري

"What is given in humiliation will be retrieved in disgrace."

—Sumerian saying

إلى سيّدي و مولاي العراق

يا سيّدي الجريح

رغماً عن أنف الموت
و ملوك الطوائف
رغماً عن أنف الريح
هاجرُ تسعى بين صفا روحك
و مروة عمرك
دجلة قِبلتُها و الحَرَمُ الفرات
بغداد عروتها الوثقى
و هواك الهوية و المرجعية

(٢٠٠٧)

To My Lord Iraq

Wounded master —

In spite of death,
the Sectarian leaders
In spite of wind

Hagar paces without end between
Safa — your soul
and Marwa — your life

The Tigris is her Mecca   The Euphrates, her Ka'ba
Baghdad, her bond   unbreaking

My lord — your love
her only identity and priest

(2007)

بلدي قبل الاحتلال

جواز سفر ممنوع من السفر

My Country Before the Occupation

Passport—travel not permitted

بلدي بعد الاحتلال

جواز سفر لخادمة فلبينية
مختوم بالأحمر
غير صالح للعراق

NOT VALID TO IRAQ

My Country After the Occupation

Passport for my Philippino maid—
red stamped:

NOT VALID TO IRAQ

الدين قبل الاحتلال

كان يقف خائفا مرتبكاً أمام عتبة الدولة.

Religion Before the Occupation

stood lost, scared
on the doorstep of the Regime

الدين بعد الاحتلال

البَسَ الدولة
سدرةً سوداء والبَسَ الدستورَ عباءة السّيد
الذي اختبأ في اللغة الفارسيّة.

Religion After the Occupation

dressed the country in black
the constitution in the robe of al-Sayed—
shroud of Persian words

أمي قبل الاحتلال

كانت تُحصي عمرَها بعددِ الراحلين
من أبنائها
فتهرب إلى الدعاء
تقيس ما تبقّى من حصّتها التموينية في الايام
فتلتحف بجوعِ الخذلان
تتطلع إلى فرحها المعطّل
تصرخ:
ألا يكفي كل ذلك
يا أيها الغائب في وهمٍ تعويذة باطلة!!؟

My Mother Before the Occupation

counted her age by the number of dead children
escaped to prayer, counting rations like days
wrapping herself in disappointment's want

Enough! she screams
at her deferred happiness

Absent savior   Useless charm

أمي بعد الاحتلال

مثل كل العجائز اضطربت أمي
حتى صارت صلاتها مرهونة بترنيمة الارتباك
لقد سئمنا هذه الديموقراطية
كان الرئيس واحدا
كان الخوف واحدا
كان الحزب واحدا
كان الحروب واحدة
كان الرعب واحدا
طعم الديمقراطية بات باهتاً
لقد مللنا هذه الديمقراطية

لم تعد عيوني قادرة على التحديق في وعودها,
شعاراتها التي ماتت في قلوبنا منذ أمد بعيد.

My Mother After the Occupation

was anxious, like all the old women
Even her prayers became a hymn
to chaos:

We're sick of you, Democracy
There used to be one president
There used to be one fear
There used to be one Party
All the wars, one war
One terror

Democracy, I lost my taste for you
Your cant rotted inside me, years ago

جارتي قبل الاحتلال

كانت أمّ حيدر تولول من اجل زيادة مرتّب زوجها
دولارين
تنام دون أن تُغلق باب بيتها
كي يدخل الهواء العذب من حديقة الجيران العاملين
في مطبخِ القصر الجمهوري.

My Neighbor Before the Occupation

Um-Hayder keened for a two-dollar raise
in her husband's check

but slept with the front door open
so the breeze could blow fresh from the garden next door
tended by cooks from the Republican Palace

جارتي بعد الاحتلال

أمّ حيدر التي ارتفع مرتّب زوجها عشرين دولاراً فجأة
لا تستطيع حتى أن تتنفّس هواء جيرانها الجدد
لأن الهواء يستطيع قراءة انتمائها الشيعي
وهي التي حاربت أصلها عقوداً من اجل أن يزداد
المرتّب دولارا واحدا لا غير.

My Neighbor After the Occupation

Now her husband's check is twenty dollars fatter,
but Um-Hayder can't risk breathing her new neighbor's air—
it will sense her Shi'ite scent, hidden for decades
just to have one dollar more

ابنتي قبل الاحتلال

كانت تسألني عن سببٍ وجودنا في بلد أُسمّيه منفى
وتُسمّيه بلادي
تقول إذا كان السَّوادُ بلادنا فلماذا هَجَرتِ بلادي
سقطت كلّ أجوبتي في
أسئلتها حتى ضاعت بلادها وهُجِّرت بلادي.

My Daughter Before the Occupation

used to ask me why we were here
I called it *exile*   She called it *my country*

She says *If Iraq is our Iraq, why did you abandon our home?*
All my answers dropped into her questions
until her country was squandered   and mine: diaspora

ابنتي بعد الاحتلال

لا تعرف غير جدّتها التي تجعّدت أكثر مما تجعّد وجه
مدينتها
ولا تريد أن تعرف أكثر من ذلك.

My Daughter After the Occupation

knows no one but her grandmother
whose face has more wrinkles than the city's

And that's all she wants to know

زوجي قبل الاحتلال

كان مترّددا بين رعبه وقلبه
كان يسمّيني أَمةً
ويُسمّى غريمتي السيّدة
كان اسمه وشماً لمحنتي
كان تاريخه محرقة لقصائدي
كان ياما كان
كان زوجي قبل الاحتلال.

My Husband Before the Occupation

He stumbled between his fear and his fire
He called me *slave*   but my opponent *lady*

His name, my tattoo of pain
His past, a Holocaust for my words

Once upon a time, my husband—

زوجي بعد الاحتلال

قلت لزوجي الذي كان من قبل أخي
لن نحتفل بالحبّ   ولن نضمخَ سرير زواجنا بالفرح
لأن «المجاهدين» الذين دخلوا حياتنا
سوف يشمّون رائحة الحب
ويقرّرون قطع رؤوس كلّ الأزواج الذين يشبهوننا.

My Husband After the Occupation

I said to my husband
who had been like a brother to me —
Let's not wet our marriage bed with one drop of happiness

The Mujahideen, now in our house,
would smell love's musk, our sweat

They'd behead anyone
who had both love and breath

الرجال قبل الاحتلال

كانوا عشاقا وزنادقة
فلاحين تلامذةً للشجر
كانوا أبطالاً على قدر ما تكذب الأخبار

Men Before the Occupation

They were lovers
gigolos   farmers
students of trees
Such heroes

as the TV made them out to be

الرجال بعد الاحتلال

لا احد يعرف من هم الرجال
ملثّمون
· في سيرك لحفل موت رجولة
خصتها كلّ عناوينِ الدم

Men After the Occupation

Who are the real men?
No one knows

Disguises lauding
the demise of manhood

A circus
wild with masks

and castration
Running blood

روحي قبل الاحتلال

كانت موؤودة في مدافن البُعد
حبلى بالمخلص في أنابيب عاقرة.

My Soul Before the Occupation

was buried alive in the grave of exile
carried the savior in a barren womb

روحي بعد الاحتلال

صارت تتوارى بين جدران المنطقة الخضراء,
صارت غطاء سماء مقفلة على التحسّر
تداري اصفرارَ نسغها الذي بدأت تأكله العائلة,
صراخ الأطفال وقبلات الزوج.

My Soul After the Occupation

escapes behind the walls of the Green Zone
that canopy sky, that stockade for regret

I hide my exhaustion, my yellowing blood
from my children's cries   my husband's caress

جسدي قبل الاحتلال

كان حشوةَ يورانيوم لاسلحةٍ مطلّقة
كان ذخيرة لحروب قادمة
كان رغيفا
ساخنا يبحث عن معدة خاوية.

My Body Before the Occupation

— Uranium for weapons, disarmed
Ammunition for wars to come
A loaf of hot bread

aching to be eaten

جسدي بعد الاحتلال

،لا يصل إلى حدود غبطته
معوق نصفُ ميتٍ يكرهُ لهاثه الأخير.

My Body After the Occupation

—Unable to reach heights of pleasure
Disabled little deaths

I hate their crowning moans

قبري قبل الاحتلال

لم يحلم بأكثر من أن يشمّ ترابَ طفولته
لم يحلم بأكثر من غطاء لفضيحةِ مماته.

My Grave Before the Occupation

never wished for anything but to smell the earth of his childhood
never wished for more than to cover the indecent face of death

قبري بعد الاحتلال

صار الموت يسأل عن هوية روحي وعن فصيلةِ طائفتي
وكأنّ الترابَ يريد أن يعرف انتسابي إليه!!

My Grave After the Occupation

started asking me whether I'm Sunni or Shi'ite
as if the dirt needs to know if I belong to him!

دجلة قبل الاحتلال

واقف في مكانه، ممنوع من السفر
تحيطه عيونُ القصر الجمهوري
التي أربكت طفولته بنظراتها المزورة.

The Tigris Before the Occupation

stagnant, forbidden to travel

by the Palace, by spying eyes
that confused her childhood

with lies

دجلة بعد الاحتلال

هجر ماءه هرباً من عيونِ المنطقة الخضراء
التي اختلطت ببرودة عيون القصر الجمهوري
وهمرات الغزاة
هرب الماء إلى العطش
ومُنِحَ جوازَ سفرٍ إلى المجهول.

The Tigris After the Occupation

escapes

the Green Zone's eyes
the Palace's eyes
the invader's grunts

running toward thirst—
a visa to the unknown

الحرية قبل الاحتلال

الرجال ينتظرون الحرية
فقد ملّوا ممارسةَ عاداتهم السريّة
في مواعيد مؤجّـلة
النساء ينتظرن الحرية
لكي يوقفن مراسيم دفنِ الأيام
الأطفال بانتظار الحرية
لكي يخبّئوا طفولاتهم في حقائبها المثقلة بالأمل

Freedom Before the Occupation

Men waited—bored
of masturbating, being stood up

Women waited—anxious
to stop burying their labored days

Children waited—desperate
to pack their youth in suitcases
lined with trust

الحرية بعد الاحتلال

تباع في المزاد
بأعلى سعر للثأر
أحزاباً وطوائف
وجارك اللئيم يرفع سعر احتضارك
ويشتري قتلاك
في سوق الحرية
- وأنت طفل ما عندك ذنب غير انك عراقي -
تباع صباحاتك لحزام ناسف
وتُوقفُ لياليك في الأسر
منعوا التجول في أحلامك
و تركوك وحيداً
تبيعك الشعاراتُ إلى اليأس
في سوقِ الحرية
كلمات لم تعرفها أيامك
مفخّخات
فرق الموت

Freedom After the Occupation

Auctioned off to the highest bidder—
revenge

Sectarian Religion, Politics
and the country next door raises the price on your head
cashing out the body

—Little you, guilty only of being Iraqi—

In the name of freedom

In a free market
all your mornings are sold for a suicide bomb
Your nights taken into custody
Your curfew enforced in your dreams
and you, left alone

In a free market
slogans sell you
in exchange for desperation
words your days never knew:
car bombs
militias

انتحاريون لا تعرف من يكونون
باسم الحرية

ـ وأنت طفل ما عندك ذنب غير انك عراقي ـ

suicide bombers
You don't know who they are

In the name of freedom

—Little you, guilty only of being Iraqi—

الشرف قبل الاحتلال

كان الشرف أن تعبد "القائد"
وتحبّ "الحزب"
وتلعن أمريكا والحصار.

Honor Before the Occupation

Worship the Leader
Love the Party
Curse America, the siege

الشرف بعد الاحتلال

أن تلعن الطاغية
وتُعلن براءتك من الحزب
وتصفق بالورد لأمريكا والجدار.

Honor After the Occupation

Curse the Dictator
Forsake the Party
Clap with flowers in your hand for America, her wall

فمي قبل الاحتلال

كان يومئ بـ اللّا وهو يرتعدُ من الهمس
كانت شفتاك تدلانني على المحنة
وتطبقان عليُّ باحتجاجك الملعون الذي خرج مني
الى الأبد.

My Mouth Before the Occupation

tried to say *no*, but couldn't
I was afraid

Instead, my tongue led me to this curse:
protests that silenced me

then seeped from me, eternal

فمي بعد الاحتلال

يصرخ بـ اللّا دونما خوف ولكنه يشعر ان شفتيه
مرهونتان قيد الاعتقال
خوف ضياع ملامح شفتيَّ التين غابتا في موتِ شفتيك.

My Mouth After the Occupation

shouts *No!* Fearless,
though my tongue fears arrest

I'm terrified of losing truth
and look—it's already gone

Exiled with God's tongues

الساعة التاسعة قبل الاحتلال

إلى المعلم الأرياني

كانت نشوةُ الجنرال تصعد إلى خالقها
تتطاول عليه
وتسخر من الغياب
والغدر
كان الخلودُ وشمَ الساعة التاسعة.

Nine O'Clock Before the Occupation

The Dictator's euphoria rose to his Maker—
his audacity above him like laughter
Who will betray me? I will never leave

His words   needles, ink
Nine o'clock his scar

الساعة التاسعة بعد الاحتلال

استيقظ الجنرال من غبطته
وهو يتطلع الى ساحة الفردوس غير مصدق ان صاحبه
فر من الجبروت إلى الجبن
وانّ الجموع التي تهلّل للزعماء تركلهم في كلّ هتاف
حدّق في عقارب الساعة
واقسم أن يدير الوقت
يُسقط أصنامه
ويرجم ساعة عمره
قبل حلول الساعة التاسعة.

Nine O'Clock After the Occupation

The Dictator wakes from his revelry,
looks out at Firdos Square

Overnight a tyrant became a coward
Overnight the crowds who'd hailed his name
were now kicking him with each chant

He checks his watch, swears
he will turn back its hands—
overturning his own idols
stoning himself

before nine o'clock comes

الندم قبل الاحتلال

كان الندم حالةً طارئةً في حياة أهلي
كان الندم حالة الذهول في قلبي
كان الندم يغمض عينيه على أخطائنا
ويمضي باحثاً عن قُوته اليومي في حصار لا ينتهي،
لا يكبر ولكنه يشيخ.

Regret Before the Occupation

A foreigner to my people—
I was stunned when he became one of us

His eyes closed, blind to our mistakes,
finding his sustenance endless in this endless siege

Regret did not change but o   how he aged

الندم بعد الاحتلال

الحرية التي جاء بها القادمون فَضّت بكارةَ الأوطان وحبل الرجال قبل نسائهم بندم يكبر ويتجدّد ولكن دون أن يشيخ.

Regret After the Occupation

Freedom, that gift from others   rapes all the virgin countries
Our men, pregnant before our women

with regret   endless in its change   ageless in its days

الوحشة قبل الاحتلال

الوحشة أسيرةُ أسرّتنا
الوحشة أسيرة أسرارنا
الوحشة مخبأ جزعنا
وعجزنا من المألوف
الوحشة أكلتنا ولكنها أبقت لنا بيوتاً نعود إليها
و سريراً نباغت أجسادنا فيه
مثل فريسةٍ في جوف ضوء يحتضر.

Loneliness Before the Occupation

arrested our sleep
our secrets
our restlessness

became a shelter
a home to return to
a bed

that ambushed us

Living prey into a stomach
The agonizing light

الوحشة بعد الاحتلال

هربت الوحشة
من الأسرّة إلى السرائر
من اليقين إلى الظلام
من عيون تبوح بالغيب
إلى شفاه حرة تُسند ملامح القبلات
الوحشة في القلوب
في الحدود
في الأزقة
في الارتباك
الوحشة نُهبت في سوقِ الضمائر
فلم يبقَ غير وحشة
دون نبضٍ،
دون ضميرٍ.

Loneliness After the Occupation

escapes from our beds to our bodies
from eyes that reveal what no human knows
to liberated lips strong in allure

Loneliness of my breast
of borders
of alleyways
of my confusion

in this market of conscience,
you are looted

Left—
without virtue
without pulse

الصور قبل الاحتلال

الصور حفنةٌ من أكاذيب
نعرف بعدها أن وجوهنا ستبقى في كيميائها
ولن تغادر إلا بتفويضٍ من سلطة الإطار
الصور
صندوق توفير نودعه طفولتنا وبطولاتنا
ونحاربُ فيه خساراتنا
الصور
رصيدُ شباب لشيخوخةٍ قادمة.

Photographs Before the Occupation

We were sure our faces would live on
in your silver light, your tyrant frames

Deposit box—
with you, we fought against all we lost:
our youthful balance, valor,

our vigor, saved
for those aged days
soon to come

الصور بعد الاحتلال

الصور عاطلةٌ عن العمل

تقف في مزابل الموت
لوحة إعلان
بوصلة تدلنا على وجوه قتلانا
تلك الصور
غادرت حدودَ هوياتنا
إلى حقائب منافينا الضائعة.

Photographs After the Occupation

We stand in dumpsters where the dead are thrown

Our only job? Follow these maps to the faces
Beloved faces, exploded Gone

Pictures—leaving the self's border
packed into a suitcase The exile: grief

العيد قبل الاحتلال

كان العيد يوحّدنا في تراتيل أمّ كلثوم
"الليلة عيد، عالدنيا سعيد"
دون أن يتشظّى في محرقة هويّاتنا.

Eid Before the Occupation

How we came together
in the hymns of Umm Kulthum
singing *Tonight — the feast*
that brings peace to all the world

No diaspora   No holocaust
for our homelands

العيد بعد الاحتلال

نحاول أن نجرّ العيدَ إلى سواد بيوتنا
نكذبُ على اطفالنا
وندّعي أننا سنذهب وإياهم إلى مدينةِ الألعاب
أو الأشباح لا فرق
صدّقونا حتى انكفأنا على صباحٍ مثقل بهدايا شوارعنا

صرخنا بأطفالنا الذين ذهبوا كلهم إلى الغياب يعانقون العيد
في ساحاتٍ لم يقطفوا منها غيرَ أكاذيبنا والعيد البعيد.

Eid After the Occupation

We drag happiness to our dark homes
We lie to our children —
Let's go to the City of Toys
But if we said the City of Ghosts
would it make a difference?

Trusting us, they wake from dreams
about what gifts the streets will bring
And though we shout, they all run out to hug
what they think will be bliss

They go, and our calls catch nothing but their absence
Our hands sort nothing but our own lies
and the unreachable Eid

الحب قبل الاحتلال

كان يلبس زيّ الشرق مرًّ
وتارةً يرتدي أزياء الغرب الأنيقة
كان أعمى لا يبصر غير سريرٍ في آخر الممرّ
وأجندة باردة
لا تتبدل أوراقها إلا بمواعيد كاذبة
ينام فيه الغرب خائفاً من شرقٍ يريد خلوداً
في عقل غرب لا يعرف من الحب إلا نزوة ولكنها غبر
عابرة.

Love Before the Occupation

wore Eastern robes one day
and Western elegance the next

Love saw nothing
but a bed at the end of a hall
a calendar cold with aborted dates

Love slept

The West trembling at the East
The East begging from the West:
Kingdom Come

Love! The West knows only whims
O—Eternal One

الحب بعد الاحتلال

مفلساً وخاسراً أراد الشرقُ تغيير معادلة الحب
أراد أن يصهر الروح في الخيال
أراد الغرب أن يسجّل براءة اختراع في مهنة الحب
لكن الشرق أغلق مختبر القلب وأعلن
عدم صلاحية الغرب للأبدية.

Love After the Occupation

left the East wanting
to change its equation,
to bind fantasy with soul

The West issues its patent
but the East, impatient,
locks the lab, leaves a sign:

The West just isn't made to last

كرة القدم قبل الاحتلال

كنا نخاف حبها
نرتعبُ من الخسارة
كانت توأم القهر وأقبية التعذيب السرّي
كان صوت مؤيد البدري يتلاشى وجرأة رعد حمودي تهرب الى
نفسها
كانت الكرة كرهنا للتسلّط واحتكار النشوة في اسم
أولاد الرئيس.

Soccer Before the Occupation

was torture

We were scared to cheer
but terrified we might lose

Moaed al-Badry, silenced
The daring of Raed Hmoudy, gone

How would we celebrate?
Even our thrill was controlled

Only the President's sons were cheering:
brother sponsors of our game, our rage

كرة القدم بعد الاحتلال

أخجلت الساسة
ووضعتهم في زنازين شعاراتهم
وأسقطت
عراق شيعستان
عراق سنّستان
رفعت في قلوبنا درجاتِ الأمل,
ركلت اليأس برمية جانبية,
وطعنت التقسيمَ بالضربة القاضية.

Soccer After the Occupation

humiliates politicians
jails them inside their own slogans
abolishes
    Shi'itistan
    Sunnistan
and free kicks our divisions

One voice—
we cheer and cheer and cheer

الموت قبل الاحتلال

كنا نتبارى في البكاء
وإقامةِ الولائم
كان العزاء هو ثقوب الغفران
والمباهاة بمدّ الأيادي إلى البطون
كان الموتُ موعداً لعناق الثابت في ذنوبنا المتحوّلة.

Death Before the Occupation

—A competition to see who could cry more
who could make the most food for those who grieved

All that moaning, it shot holes into Heaven's grace
while we ate from the banquet, insatiable and smiling

And what would deliver us from sin?
The day of our death   that fast embrace

الموت بعد الاحتلال

ختم احمر على فم
مدينة أُصيبت بانفلونزا الطائفية
الموت دكتاتور البلاد الأوحد
وزواج المتعة
الذي ورث كل زواجات المسيار في عمر البلاد.

Death After the Occupation

—A red mask over the mouth
of a city infected with Sectarian Flu

The only dictators in the country:
death and Nikah Misyar

an hour's contract
taking all life contracts, all other loves

العظام قبل الاحتلال

الى كارين

هي حرب ازلية بين فتنة كلوباترا
وجماد عظامها
كانت تتباهى بعتمةِ السواد في عينيها
واتساع شفتيها لأكاذيب الرجال
وطول شعرها الذي كان ملاءةً يلتحفُ بها العالم
كانت تسخر من ملامح البشر
وتتباهى بخلود شهوتها في معركة الأبدية
زعماء بلادها اتعبوا المرمر في خلق ظلالهم فوق الريح
تذكرة بأبديتهم الطارئة
كانوا يظنون
ان اصنامهم ستدرأ ء عنهم شماتة القبور
كانت العظام تسخر من هذا كله
تحاول أن تصيح : خذوني بدل الحجر
أنا وشمكم الخالد
خذوني بدل أبراجكم الكاذبة
خذوني بدل حروبكم الساقطة

Bones Before the Occupation

—an everlasting war
between Cleopatra's charms
and her stone-still bones

How she flirted with night
her large black eyes
her flush lips absorbing men's lies
her long hair swaddling the world

And while she crowed, her lust
undying in its combat against age,
the Empire wasted her marble
casting shadows to the wind—

as if a rock could keep the grave from gloating

And the bones, mocking all of it, said:
Take me, instead—I will never break or tumble
Take me instead of illusory towers
instead of your wars

I am your inheritance
I am your ancestor
Nothing, no one remains but me

أنا التي بقيت من عهد أجدادكم
أكلت موتاكم ولم يبق الآي
الشمس تخافني والقمر يهرب من طقطقتي
والهواء يدخلني هارباً من قامتي
والماء يغسلُ هشاشةَ التراب والغبار ويطرد انفاس
الغرباء لازداد بهاءً
الكل أتباعي وأنا ربة البقاء
خذوني جمعوني سأدلّكم على تجارة بقائكم الخاسرة
لأنكم تفسخّتم قبل ظهوري وتجمّعت في غيابكم
اعد موتاي.

The sun fears me
The moon runs scared of my clacking
Air gusts

And I am washed clean of dust and the breath of strangers

Follow me   I am the goddess of the infinite:
Gather me, take me—

I will point you toward your poor investment
I will count for you how, in forgetting unity,
you let death come and take you
How many, how many for whom death came

العظام بعد الاحتلال

العظام تسأل أين دمي؟
وتعوي في وادي السلام

لا تبتعدوا إن العراق مقبرةٌ تقترب...
لا تموتوا هناك إن الأوطان تمشي إليكم...

Bones After the Occupation

—a wail in the Valley of Peace:
Do we die for nothing?

Don't go far, Iraq   A cemetery is approaching
Don't die there   The homelands are coming to you

هاجر قبل الاحتلال

كانت تريد العودة
لتعثر على أجوبةٍ لأحلامها القديمة
هل بقي ماء دجلة زمزم؟
وهل بقي العشّاق بانتظار الفرات؟
كانت تطفئ نار الحرب بأردانها وتصرخ
حذارِ الحروب
هي سوط أعمى

حاذروا خياناتها
الحرب بائعةُ هوى
لا يهمّها سوى ثمن مدفوع سلفاً.

Hagar Before the Occupation

She wanted to come home so she asked
for directions from the ancients in her dreams:

Is the Tigris still as pure as Zamzam?
Do lovers still look for each other at the Euphrates?

The fires of war—
she tried to put them out with her own sleeves
She shouted:

Watch yourselves! War is a blind lash—
War is a whore
She doesn't care about anyone
Just her price, paid up-front

هاجر بعد الاحتلال

سَقَطت الأقنعة كلّها
وهاجر تبحث عن وجهها القديم
الشوارع معصوبةُ الأعين.

هاجرُ هَجَرَت هجرَها
وهَجّرت حياتها إلى اجلٍ تسمّيه الوطن ويُطلق عليه
الآخرون
أضغاث أحلام.

ليس من احد سواها
أمامها احتلال ووراءها احتلال
وما بينهما
تلك
الحرية اللقيطة.

Hagar After the Occupation

All the masks fall
as she searches for her old face

but the streets wear blindfolds

Hagar—she abandons her life
Hagar—she is a martyr for her home,
what others called a dust-filled dream

There is no one but Hagar
Before her, the Occupation
Behind her, the Occupation

And freedom?
A bastard child
An orphan

Without a name

بغداد قبل الاحتلال

كانت وحشتي التي أعود إليها
أخبّيء ديني السرّي في مكتباتها
أعود واسند راسي على كتفها فتقرأ ملامح تعبي
وتدثّرني بنسيم حدائقها فاحلم بين عينيها
بحماقتي
و قصيدتي
دمعتي التي سبقتني إليها.

Baghdad Before the Occupation

—My solitude, to which I always returned
City that kept my secret religion in her libraries

I came back to rest my head on her shoulder
and with just one look, she saw how tired I was

She wrapped her gardens, her fragrance, around me
She warmed me and in her eyes I saw
how stupid I'd been

My poems were tears that reached my beloved
long before I did

بغداد بعد الاحتلال

منطقة حمراء
تلبس عمامةً ووجهَ ملثَّم يأكل أهلها
ومنطقة خضراء
تعلن انهزام المرتزقة
ومعسكر ازدهار
يعلن خراب البلاد
ومعسكر شرف
يعلن سقوط الشرف
ومعسكر حرية
يعلن عبوديتنا ضمن قانون طوارئ لا ينتهي إلا بموت
العراق.

Baghdad After the Occupation

—A Red Zone:
City of killers wearing turbans and black masks

—A Green Zone:
City announcing that the killers are gone

And Camp Izdehar (Camp Prosperity)
announcing *Devastation*

And Camp Sharaf (Camp Honor)
announcing *Humiliation*

And Camp Huria (Camp Freedom)
announcing our enslavement

in a police state that will never end
so long as there is an Iraq

باب الاناشيد

THE CANTOS CHAPTER

انتحار السؤال

يا ربّة الحزن
يا ربّة الجروح
يا ربّة الصبر
مكسورةً مهجورةً تنزفين
يعلو أيامك الغبار
والحرائق تطفيء قلبك الحزين
بغداد
بغداد
اهلك أحبوك حبا بربرياً
ولأنك الجلاد والضحية
أبدلوا موتهم برحيل الطغاة
لا لا الحرب لم تكن هناك
الحرب كانت ها هنا
في قلوب الامهات
في
كآبة الأطفال
في سقوطك

The Suicide

O—

Goddess of Sorrow
Goddess of Wounds
Goddess of Endurance

Broken Abandoned Bleeding
Plumes of dust rise above your days
Fires put out your sad heart

Baghdad
Baghdad

Your people loved you the way barbarians love
You, who are both abuser and victim
They exchange their own lives for your release

No—
No—

The War was never there
The War was right here:
In the mother's heart
In the grief-struck child

في سجونك
في انتحار السؤال
اهلك أحبوك
حبا بربرياً
ولأنك الجلاد والضحية أبدلوا موتهم برحيل الطغاة
حتى غدوت للغزاة
لست بعيدةً وللعاشقين جدّ بعيدة
بغداد بغداد يا بغداد.

In your defeat
In your prisons

Your people loved you
A Barbarian Love

And because you are both abuser and victim
They sacrificed their lives for your release

Until you were so close
To the invaders
But to your lovers
So far

Baghdad
Baghdad

O—
Baghdad

يا دجلة الذكريات

الى روح الشهيد عثمان ابن علي

يادجلة الذكريات

يا أمَّ الكربلاءات
يا أمَّ الأنين...
تحييك أجساد جسر الأئمة – وفواجع الأمة
وهذه الخيبات
وظلم الطغاة
والظلاميّون القادمون

يا مدناً تأكل أبناءها
كي تخبّئهم بعيدا عن
الغزاة والمجهول والقدر اللعين
يا أمَّ الذاكرة...
ناسية أبناءها في مائها
ما عاد هناك فرق بين
سمك ميت على جرفها

O Tigris

for the martyr Othman Bin Ali

O Tigris—Torrent of Memories
Mother of bloody Karbala
Mother of Moaning

The bodies on Imams Bridge salute you
As does our nation's ruin
As do all our regrets
And the tyrants' violence
And the new fundamentalists

O City—who eats her own sons
To hide them from the invaders
And from those not yet known
And from our destiny, damned

O Mother of Memory
Your forgotten sons
Drowned in your own waters

There is no difference now
Between the desperate throngs
Wailing over life, wishing for death
And the dead fish on your banks

وحشود تندب الحياة وتشتهي الممات

مثل حظ العراقيين

. . . .

بكى الله ولم يبكِ

بموت ابنك

موته نار برد وسلام

على عمر البلاد

على عمر العراق

الواحدُ الأحد

لم يولد سنيّا

لم يولد شيعياً

عراق سومري

عراق بابلي

عراق عربي

Such is the luck of the Iraqis

God cried
And God did not cry
For your son's death—

A cold fire of comfort
For our countries
For the life of Iraq

The One and only One
Was not born Sunni
Was not born Shi'ite

Iraq   Sumeria
Iraq   Babylon
Iraq   Arabia

ياسيد البيت الابيض

يا سيّد البيت الأبيض
اعد لي مدينتي بلا نعوش
اعد لي مدينتي بلا سواد

اعد لي تلك البلاد
التي كانت تُسمّى يوماً بلادي
"موطني موطني"
. . . .

كانت الحرية في سبات
وحينما جاءت
جاء التطرف
تناسل العنف
كبر الموت - كبر الخوف
وتعدّد الطغاة
"لا نريد لا نريد
موطناً يُرَمّد وفتيةً تُشَرّد

To the Master of the White House

O—

Give me back my city
Without caskets
Without clothes of grief

Give me back the country
That once was called my country

My homeland
My homeland

Freedom was deep in sleep
And when it awoke
Fundamentalism came
Violence begat violence
Death ballooned
Fear ballooned
Tyrants bred

We refuse
We refuse

لانريد لانريد"

يا سيّد البيت الأبيض

. . . .

لا لست المسيح

كل القتلى تصيح

هنا في بلادي . . . هناك في بلادك

وحق موطني

لا لن اغفر لك

. . . .

يا سيّد البيت الأبيض

" لن نكون للعدا كالعبيد كالعبيد"

عد من حيث أتيت

كل القتلى تصيح

لا لن اغفر لك

عد من حيث انتهيت

يا سيد البيت الأبيض

" موطني موطني"

A *homeland turned to ashes*
A *homeless child born*

We refuse
We refuse

O—Master of the White House
I am not Jesus Christ
Here in my country
There, in yours
All the slain cry out

I swear to my homeland
I will not forgive you

O—Master of the White House

Slaves we will never be
Never slaves to our enemies

Draw back   Draw back
All the slain cry out:

We will not forgive you
We will not forgive you
Draw back

O—Master of the White House

My homeland
My homeland

كلنا خاسرون

آه آه لم تَحترق وحدها بغداد
لم تَسقط وحدها وحدها بغداد
لم تُسلب وحدها وحدها بغداد
آه آه لم تُخطف وحدها بغداد
لم تَنزف وحدها وحدها بغداد
لم تقتل وحدها وحدها بغداد
كلّنا خاسرون كلّنا خاسرون
يا سيّدي العراق
وحدها لم تحترق وحدها بغداد
وحدها لم تسقط وحدها بغداد
وحدها لم تُسلب وحدها بغداد
وحدها لم تخطف وحدها بغداد

We All Lost

Baghdad did not burn alone

O—
O—

Baghdad did not fall alone alone
Baghdad was not looted alone alone

Baghdad was not kidnapped alone

O—
O—

Baghdad did not bleed alone alone
Baghdad was not killed alone alone

We all lost
We all lost

O—My Lord, Iraq

Alone Baghdad did not burn alone
Alone Baghdad did not fall alone
Alone Baghdad was not raided alone

وحدها لم تَنزف وحدها بغداد
وحدها لم تُقتل وحدها بغداد
كلّنا خاسرون
يا سيّدي العراق

Alone Baghdad was not kidnapped alone
Alone Baghdad did not bleed alone
Alone Baghdad was not killed alone

We all lost

O—My Lord, Iraq

وداعا أيها الشعر

FAREWELL, POETRY

الشعر قبل الاحتلال

كنت عينيّ الواسعتين تدلانني إلى بلدي

كنت بوصلتي التي تدل برلينَ إلى حاراتِ بغداد
كنت حبلَ مشيمتي التي قذفت بي إلى حتفي
كنت مخلوقتك بل كنت ربتك

كنت وريثتك وكنت عبدي والإله

كنت سماوياً كما كنت
كنت عشيقي الغادر
كنت رقما وخصما يشير إلى العدم

Poetry Before the Occupation

Your beckoning eyes guided me
to my country

bringing Berlin to the streets
of Baghdad

Before the womb expelled me
you were my cord to the placenta

I was your creation
No—your goddess

I, your heiress
You, my slave
You, my god

You came from Paradise
and so did I

My cheating lover
A number, a zero-sum

هكذا ظنّوك خاسرَ حرب
ظلّ طريقَ الهزيمة
إلى مقاومة ميتة

That's why people mistook you
for the one who lost the war

You lost the way—caught
in a dead resistance

الشعر بعد الاحتلال

أصبحتَ مهاناً غيرَ قادر على حَملِ وحشتي

أصبحت عبئاً على موتي
وتحولت نخّاسا يبيعُ ذكرياتي ويغتابُ روحي ويدل
الغرباءَ على أوراقي
لا لستَ أنت
وكذلك لست أنا تغير العالم من حولنا
تغيرنا أو كنا كذلك دون أن ندري
لقد توهمتك كل تلك السنين
جمعتني في فمك وشاياتٍ لحكاياتٍ ناقصة
وجبرت روحي بالصبر وبالانتظار الذي ظل وشمي واناي
لكنك ضيعت بكارة روحي في أكاذيب وعودك
أكلتني جائعاً وصمت خائفةً عليك
ما الذي جَنيتُ منك
غير حُسّاد دخلوا موسوعة غينس بإعدادهم وأحقادهم
غير عشّاق مغلوبين على مُرّهم
يكذبون ليتسلقوا الطريقَ إليك

Poetry After the Occupation

Weighted with shame, you became
too weak to hold my grief

So heavy my death
could not hold you,

a slaver trading my memories
bidding my papers to strangers

No
Not you

And not me, either
The world changed around us

Or were we like this
the whole time and blind?

All these years, I thought
I knew you

I was wrong

أيها الشعر أيها المراوغ والمخادع

بناتك عاهرات

اجل كل القصائد التي تظن أنها ستغوي روحي بالعودة

وسفك ساعات الوقت

ما أنت إلا أرذل الأرباب يا ربّ الشعر

لستُ جاحدةً هباتك حينما كنت سمساراً شريفاً بيني

وبين الله

لكنك عدت وصرت حجاباً

بين الخلاص وبين أُذن ربك التي أُصيبت بالصمم

لم تعد قادراً على صون شرف قصائدك

حينما انتحرت صرخاتُ أهلي عند أسوارك

لقد متّ، اجل حينما عفتك خاسراً

وحيداً لا تملك غير تاريخ من الخوفِ والمدائح

سأخونك مثلما أوقعت بي وأصبحت أسيرتك كل تلك

الاعوام

في زنزانتك الرخيصة المسماة ''القصيدة''

وفي سجنك العقيم المسمّى ''شاعرة''

سجنك الذي شابه أبي غريب في ساديّة الأسرى والسجّانين

الضحايا سجّانون

والسجّانون ضحايا وعودك الغريبة يا أبا الغريب

You gathered me into your mouth,
a spy speaking half-truths

You plastered my fractured soul
with patience

until all I knew to do
was wait for you

My innocence, raped
Your promises, hollow and looting—

You were hungry
so you ate me

while I feared for you
and fasted

What have I earned?

Other than enemies who merit a world record
in number and malice

Other than lovers, seducing me
so they can have you

Oh, poetry
Oh, sly cheat

Your daughters are whores
You think they can tempt me

كنت ديني السرّي

أسرفت كثيراً في علمانيتك وعرّيت وصايانا للغرباء

ونحن العزّل لا نقدر أن ندرأ مصائرنا أو نمد اكفّنا

لنُوقفَ نهبَ هباتنا وفردوسنا

عبثاً كنت أحاول أن امشي وحريتي باتجاه غيومك علها

تمطر على شعبي بالسلام

كنت بخيلاً

كلما اقتربتُ من غيمك سارعت لا بل هربت وتركتني

أسيرةَ الشمس

لم كلّ هذا الصحو

لا أريد نهارك لأنه يفضي إلى العطش لأنه لا يفضي إلا

إلى العطش

أنا الحبلى بالذكريات

أنا الخالقة للحكايا

قل لي

اخبرني متى سيجيء الليل

فانا منذ دهر بانتظار الهلال

أريده عرافاً قبل أن يكتمل ويكمل معه غيابي الأخير

أو ظهوري لا فرق

لا أريده بدرا لأنه سيضيء العتمة وأنا أصلّي للظلام

هذا احتجاجي هذا عبثي

and I will return to you,
letting my hours like blood

You are the lowest of gods—

I won't deny what you once offered me
when you were honest

my arbiter of the Divine

But you became a wall
between deliverance

and your god's ear, deaf
Your word, already lost

My family's wails, suicides
hidden in your stones

When I left, you were dead, alone
holding nothing

but the past,
its terror and praise—

So I will betray you
just as you betrayed me

All those years, a set up
to bring me captive

أيها المهزومُ ترجّل عن جوادك من صمتك
كنت نمراً من ورقٍ مزوّر
لا لست أنت من يشدّ ألمي باتجاه أن ينمو رحمي
بالغلة ويطيل قامتي
أنت قزم لا تليق
بهاجر حملت الله جريحاً معها كلّ هذا الدهر

أصبحت شارةً للشيطانِ ولعنةَ الشرق
حاولتُ أن أُدخلك خانة الحياد لكنك بقيت فَحلاً في
ضميرك النحوي
كنت (عمودياً) في زمن كان اهلُك سادة الكون
ثم تكسّرت قليلاً فأصبحت (حُراً)
ولكنك تشظيت حتى لم يبق منك إلا هذا (النثر) أو
الندم.

136

your cheap cell called *Poem*
your barren prison called *Poet*

your prison, this Abu Ghraib
where all are sadists

the inmates, jailers   the jailers, inmates
of your strange promises

O you, father of strangers —

My secret religion,
now profane

exposing us, unarmed
unable to defend against fate

unable to war
against the spoil

of our bounty,
our paradise

What a waste —

I used to walk, head in the clouds
thinking, *Maybe peace will rain upon my people*

But whenever I came to look for you,
you'd drift

deserting me to be
the sun's hostage

What use do I have for his clarity?
I don't want the day

It leads to thirst
It leads only to thirst

I am the progenitor of stories
I am pregnant with memory

Tell me
Tell me

When will night come?
I have waited ages

for the crescent moon, my oracle,
to come before becoming full

I want her to accompany me
in my final absence

or appearance
It doesn't matter which

No, I don't want the full moon

She will light up the darkness
and I pray for darkness

This is my protest
This is my folly—

Defeated, you step down
from your horse, silent

A tiger
A paper tiger

You are not the one
who will abate my pain

You are not the one who will stretch my womb
with a harvest of fruit and dignity

I want to walk tall
and you are a pigmy

You're not fit for Hagar

she who carried God,
wounded, all this time

You're the devil's sign
A curse on the East

A conscience, a grammar
A stud bull

that I tried to castrate

Once, you were classical verse
Once, your people ruled the world

then you broke
piece by piece,

free

You shattered
and what was left?

This prose
This regret

NOTES

"To My Lord Iraq"

According to Islamic texts, Hajar (transliterated here as "Hagar") was either the wife or the maidservant of the prophet Ibrahim and was the mother of Ismail, patriarch of Islam. In response to Sara's jealousy, Ibrahim leaves Hagar and their son in the desert of Paran which surrounds Mecca. Hagar and Ismail begin to dehydrate, and Hagar runs between the mountains Safa and Marwa praying for water. Allah rescues her when the ground springs a miraculous well known as Zamzam. Contemporary Muslims on pilgrimage walk between the two hills seven times in memory of Hagar.

Ka'ba: Located in Mecca, Ka'ba is a Muslim's most holy site.

Baghdad, her bond unbreaking: Qur'an 2:256. "Let there be no compulsion in religion: Truth stands out clear from Error: whoever rejects evil and believes in Allah hath grasped the most trustworthy hand-hold, that never breaks. And Allah heareth and knoweth all things."

"Religion After the Occupation"

al-Sayed: a title given to a high-ranking Shi'ite Muslim scholar.

"My Neighbor Before the Occupation"

The Republican Palace: the largest of the Ba'ath Party palaces.

"My Neighbor After the Occupation"

Notwithstanding the Sunni dominance of Iraqi government and culture under Ba'ath Party rule, Shi'ites had some opportunity for advancement. During the Occupation, they gained political and economic clout, but, because of the violent sectarian insurgency, Sunnis and Shi'ites together lived in a climate of greater fear.

"My Daughter Before the Occupation"

The poet fled to Europe in 1997 and settled in Münich, Germany.

"My Husband After the Occupation"

Mujahideen: literally, "freedom fighters." In Iraq the term refers to the broad insurgency.

"My Soul Before the Occupation"

was buried alive in the grave of exile: referring to female infanticide, a common practice in pre-Islamic Arabia demeaned by Mohammed through the Qur'an. Often cited is Qur'an 81: 8–9, 14: "and when the female infant buried alive is asked for what sin she was killed . . . [then] each soul shall know what it has put forward."

"My Soul After the Occupation"

The Green Zone: or the International Zone of Iraq, the area in central Baghdad that was once the administrative center for the Ba'ath Party and was taken in 2003 by Coalition forces.

"Nine O'Clock Before the Occupation"

Nine O'Clock: the time of day when Coalition forces took Firdos Square and the statue of Saddam Hussein was toppled.

"Eid Before the Occupation"

Eid ul-Fitr: a Muslim celebration that closes Ramadan.

Umm Kulthum: an Egyptian vocalist of great acclaim in the Arab world.

"Eid After the Occupation"

The City of Toys: (idiomatic) amusement parks.

"Soccer Before the Occupation"

During Ba'ath Party rule Uday Hussein, the dictator's son, directed the national team. He was notorious for threatening team members with torture if they lost.

Moaed al-Badry: a famous announcer in Iraqi sports.

Raed Hmoudy: a famous goalkeeper in Iraqi soccer.

"Soccer After the Occupation"

After the Ba'ath Party's reign ended, the Iraqi soccer team began to amass an extraordinary string of victories, which included winning the Gold Medal at the 2005 West Asian Games. In 2007 Iraq won the AFC Asian Cup and was named the AFC team of the year, *Al-Ahram's* Arab team of the year, and *World Soccer's* world team of the year.

Shi'itistan / Sunnistan: referring to the media rumor that then-Senator Joe Biden advocated in 2007 for a partitioned Iraq. If he had done so, he would have been calling for Iraq to split into three separate nations, primarily Sunni, Shi'ite, and Kurdish. In fact, he called for a federal Iraq that would include empowered regional governments.

"Death After the Occupation"

Nikah Misyar: a temporary, fixed-period marriage that is legal for Shi'ites and allows men who are traveling to enjoy sexual pleasure. It requires no further financial commitment to the woman or to any potential children after the marriage ends.

"Bones After the Occupation"

The Valley of Peace: Iraq's great Shi'ite burial ground; one of the world's largest cemeteries. More recent burials include those bodies recovered from the mass graves of Saddam Hussein's covert executions.

"Hagar After the Occupation"

A bastard child / An orphan: referring to Nikah Misyar. The poet implies that freedom is the bastard child of the temporary marriage between Iraq and the United States.

"Baghdad After the Occupation"

Red Zone: refers to the area just outside the Green Zone or to any area in Occupied Iraq unsecured by Coalition Forces.

Camp Izdehar, Camp Sharaf, Camp Huria: All areas located inside the Green Zone.

"The Suicide"

Your people loved you the way barbarians love: referring to the Siege of Baghdad, 1258. This brutal invasion by the Ilkhanate Mongol forces marked the end of the Islamic Golden Age.

Until you were so close/To the invaders/But to your lovers/So far: an adaptation of lines from Johann Wolfgang von Goethe's poem "Suleika."

"O Tigris"

Othman Bin Ali: a young Sunni martyr. A professional swimmer, he died trying to save Shi'ite pilgrims who were drowning in the Tigris River during the tragedy of al-Aimma Bridge, or the Bridge of the Imams.

Mother of bloody Karbala: The battle waged in 680 between Muhammad's grandson Hussein ibn Ali and the Sunni forces of Yazid I. Because Shi'ites believe Hussein ibn Ali was the rightful heir to Muhammed's teaching and lineage, his death remains the most significant event in Shi'ite history. Battles of Karbala also took place in 2003 and 2007. The first when American troops cleared the city of Republican guard forces; the second when the Mahdi Army fought the Iraqi police during a celebration of Mid-Sha'ban, threatening the thousands of Shi'ite pilgrims who had gathered.

The bodies on Imams Bridge salute you: The Imams Bridge spans the Tigris between two neighborhoods, one Shi'ite, one Sunni. On August 31, 2005, more than a thousand Shi'ites remembering the death of Imam Musa al-Kadhim died there in a stampede after mortar fire sounded and the rumor of a suicide bomber spread. At the time, it was the single greatest loss of Iraqi lives since the 2003 invasion. Because Sunni groups were quickly blamed, they feared Shi'ite retaliation; however, many Sunni men risked their lives to save the drowning victims and the Sunni leaders called for support on behalf of the wounded. Thus the tragedy became a symbol for possible Sunni / Shi'ite accord.

A cold fire of comfort: a reference to Qur'an 21:68–70. When the young prophet Ibrahim challenged the idol worship of his fathers, they retaliated saying, "'Burn him and help your deities, if you are resolved to do something.' But We [Allah] said, 'Fire! Be cool and a means of safety for Ibrahim.' They had sought to do him harm, but We frustrated them."

The One and only One: a reference to Qur'an 112: 1–4. "Say, 'He is God, the One, God, the Self-sufficient One. He does not give birth, nor was He born, and there is nothing like Him'."

"To the Master of the White House"

Italicized passages are from the Palestinian poet Ibrahim Touqan's *My Homeland*, considered the first national anthem of post-war Iraq.

"Poetry After the Occupation"

"Abu Ghraib," the American military prison infamous for torture, is a near rhyme to "abu gharib," which means "father of strangers." The poet uses this coincidence to conflate the two meanings for the reader of the Arabic poem.

ALICIA OSTRIKER has published thirteen poetry collections, including *The Book of Seventy*, which received the 2009 National Jewish Book Award for Poetry. *The Crack in Everything* and *The Little Space: Poems Selected and New, 1969–1989*, were both National Book Award finalists. As a critic, Ostriker has written several books on poetry and on the Bible. Ostriker is Professor Emerita of Rutgers University, and teaches in The Drew University Low-Residency MFA Program in Poetry & Poetry in Translation.

 REBECCA GAYLE HOWELL's poems and translations have appeared or are forthcoming in such publications as *Ninth Letter, Massachusetts Review, Ecotone, Indiana Review, Hayden's Ferry Review*, and *Poetry Daily*. She holds a combined MFA from Drew University and is a 2010/2011 fellow at the Fine Arts Work Center in Provincetown, MA.

 HUSAM QAISI, originally from Amman, Jordan, earned his BS in business administration from Jordan University and, after coming to the United States in 2004, earned a second BS in business administration from Sullivan University. Steeped in a love of classical Arabic verse, Qaisi is particularly influenced by the poet al-Mutanabi. When Qaisi is not traveling the globe as an executive for Qaisi Electronics, he lives in Louisville, Kentucky with his wife Vemihan and their four children.

BOOK BENEFACTORS

Alice James Books, Amal al-Jubouri, and Rebecca Howell wish to thank the following individuals, who generously contributed toward the publication of:

Hagar Before the Occupation
Hagar After the Occupation

Brian Turner

For more information about AJB's book benefactor program, contact us via phone or email, or visit us at www.alicejamesbooks.org to see a list of forthcoming titles.

RECENT TITLES FROM ALICE JAMES BOOKS

ALICE JAMES BOOKS has been publishing poetry since 1973 and remains one of the few presses in the country that is run collectively. The cooperative selects manuscripts for publication primarily through regional and national annual competitions. Authors who win a Kinereth Gensler Award become active members of the cooperative board and participate in the editorial decisions of the press. The press, which historically has placed an emphasis on publishing women poets, was named for Alice James, sister of William and Henry, whose fine journal and gift for writing went unrecognized during her lifetime.

Designed by Dede Cummings
Composition by Carolyn Kasper and Dede Cummings
DCDESIGN

Printed by Thomson-Shore
on 30% postconsumer recycled paper
processed chlorine-free